j332.024 Rissman, Rebecca.
R596s Saving money.

WITHDRAWN
MAY 2011

Money Arou[nd]

Saving Money

Rebecca Rissman

Heinemann Library
Chicago, Illinois

© 2008 Heinemann Library
a division of Reed Elsevier Inc.
Chicago, Illinois

Customer Service 888-454-2279
Visit our website at www.heinemannraintree.com

All rights reserved. No part of this publication may be reproduced or transmitted in any form or by any means, electronic or mechanical, including photocopying, recording, taping, or any information storage and retrieval system, without permission in writing from the publisher.

Designed by Joanna Hinton-Malivoire
Photo Research by Tracy Cummins and Heather Mauldin
Printed in China by Leo Paper Group

12 11 10 09
10 9 8 7 6 5 4 3 2

The Library of Congress has cataloged the first edition as follows:
Rissman, Rebecca.
  Saving money / Rebecca Rissman.
    p. cm. -- (Money around the world)
  Includes bibliographical references and index.
  ISBN-13: 978-1-4329-1070-9 (hc)
  ISBN-13: 978-1-4329-1075-4 (pb)
  1. Finance, Personal--Juvenile literature. 2. Saving and investment--Juvenile literature. I. Title.
  HG179.R542 2008
  332.024--dc22
                          2007035637

Acknowledgments
The author and publisher are grateful to the following for permission to reproduce copyright material: ©AFP p. **13** (Getty Images/ SAIF DAHLAH); ©Age Fotostock pp. **10**, **23a** (Flying Colours Ltd.), **17** (Picture Partners), **20** (Glowimages); ©Alamy pp. **5** (Peter Titmuss), **18** (Rob Walls), **19** (Peerpoint); ©CORBIS p. **6** (Ronnie Kaufman); ©Getty Images pp. **4** (Nick Dolding), **7** (AFP/Teh Eng Koon), **8** (Kristjan Maack), **11** (Robert Nickelsberg), **12**, **23b** (Don Smetzer), **14** (Yann Layma), **15** (Ken Chernus), **16**, **23c** (Zubin Shroff), **21** (Elyse Lewin), **22a** (Nick Dolding), ; ©The World Bank pp. **9**, **22b** (Eric Miller).

Cover photograph reproduced with permission of ©agefotostock (Angelika Antl).
Back cover photograph reproduced with the permission of Age Fotostock (Flying Colours Ltd).

Every effort has been made to contact copyright holders of any material reproduced in this book. Any omissions will be rectified in subsequent printings if notice is given to the publisher.

Contents

Saving Money

People can save money.

People save money to buy
things later.

People save money to buy big things.

People save money to buy
little things.

People save money for a short time.

People save money for a long time.

People save money in jars.

People save money in banks.

Needs

People save money to buy things they need.

People save money to buy food.

People save money to buy clothing.

People save money to buy homes.

Wants

People save money to buy things they want.

People save money to buy toys.

People save money to buy books.

People save money to go on trips.

Money Around the World

People save money around the world.

People save money for later.

Ways People Save Money

 ◄Money Jar

 ◄Bank

Picture Glossary

needs what people must have. Food, clothing, and housing are needs.

save to keep or store

wants what people do not need. Toys, books, and TVs are wants.

Index

Note to Parents and Teachers
Before reading: Ask children if they have ever seen a bank. Then, ask if they have a money jar at home. Prompt children to guess why people would use a bank or money jar.

After reading:
Discuss with children that people often save money to buy things later. Make a list of items that people save money to buy. Explain that some things cost more money than others. Ask children to list expensive and inexpensive goods or services.